'Parts of His Ways'

While the Candle Burns
Today—A book of devotions
Sung in Our Hearts—Studies in the Psalms
As the Sun Climbs—Autobiography
If I Open My Door
Through Open Windows
When We Two Walked
The Winds Blow
A Thousand Sunrises
The Lark is in the Sky
Safety Last—Tales of the Pacific
Prodigal of the Seven Seas—Biography
There's No Place Like Home
Trees Unafraid (Lutterworth Press)
I Turn to Ducks
Here be People
His Interpreters—Devotions
From a Hilltop
Seven Days of the Week
I Believe in the Dawn

For Children

Listen, Children!
Story-time Again
What Time is it?
Over the Hills and Home Again
The Ark at the End of the Garden
Hobson's Choice

'Lo, these are parts of his ways'

'Parts of His Ways'

A BOOK OF DEVOTIONS

BY

RITA F. SNOWDEN

'Lo, these are parts of his ways'
JOB 26:14

LONDON
THE EPWORTH PRESS

FIRST PUBLISHED IN 1958

© THE EPWORTH PRESS 1958

Book Steward
FRANK H. CUMBERS

Reprinted 1962

SET IN MONOTYPE BEMBO AND PRINTED IN
GREAT BRITAIN BY THE CAMELOT PRESS LTD
LONDON AND SOUTHAMPTON

To

LORNA

Staunch friend,
valiant spirit

O Thou, in all Thy might so far,
  In all Thy love so near,
Beyond the range of sun or star,
  And yet beside us here!

What heart can comprehend Thy name,
  Or, searching, find Thee out,
Who art within, a quickening flame,
  A presence round about.

Yet, though I know Thee but in part,
  I ask not, Lord, for more:
Enough for me to know Thou art,
  To love Thee and adore.

FREDERICK HOSMER

7

Introduction

In the beautiful city where I was a student, is a graceful building. I visited it again lately. Standing in the company of great trees, it is almost always sun-flecked. Even when one has no time to go in, the small columns of its portico, and the pattern of leaves in that pool of peace are something to remember.

It is a Museum, and owes a debt to the far-sightedness of many. But I have never been able to discover who had the genius to chisel across its portico those glorious words from Job: 'Lo, these are parts of his ways, but how little a portion is heard of him.'

'Parts of his ways.' What words could so engender the proper spirit of approach? The casual passer-by, or the careful student, who steps beneath that chiselled inscription finds himself confronted with part of the revelation of God. And if his shoes are not taken from off his modern feet because the ground whereon he treads is holy, surely something happens to his spirit.

None of us claims to know God fully—that is the significance of the inscription. All that we see are 'parts of His ways'. Nowhere—in Nature, Religion or Art—can we say: 'All of God is here!' He is so much more than any part of His creation.

But the whole wondrous universe proclaims Him

9

—fastening the mighty planets in their courses, fashioning the tiniest seed with mathematical exactness. Of these things, great and small, Sir Bertram Windle says: 'There is no middle course; they must be the product of mechanical forces acting at random, or they must be the ordinances of an Intelligent Law-Giver.'

> This is a piece too fair
> To be the child of Chance, and not of Care.
> No atoms casually together hurl'd
> Could e'er produce so beautiful a world.

Those glorious words across the portico, may be inscribed across the world.

They may be inscribed as reverently and meaningfully, across the Old and New Testaments. From the very beginning, God had delighted to reveal to His children, 'parts of His ways'. But at best, they have been only parts.

And in this strange modern life that we live—mingling our secret hopes and our secret shames—we may as meaningfully write these words across our history and friendship and human love and humble service. That is the purpose of this slender book.

R. F. S.

Contents

Illustrations

'From Apparent Death'—Life

'From Apparent Death'—Life

Now the full-throated daffodils,
  Our trumpeters in gold,
Call resurrection from the ground
  And bid the year be bold

C. DAY LEWIS

(*Thanksgiving and Praise*)

After the bleak days of winter, God is saying something to me:

Through this lovely picture—

Through my own experience of Spring—

Through the words of Scripture—

> For, lo, the winter is past,
> The rain is over and gone;
> The flowers appear on the earth.
>
> SONG OF SOLOMON 2:11-12

> Behold, I will do a new thing; now it shall spring forth. ISAIAH 43:19

Through the joyful note of the hymn-writer—

> 'O Lord of every lovely thing.'
> 'For the beauty of the earth.'
> 'All creatures of our God and King.'

Through the glad confidence of the poet—

> None can hold back the Spring,
> The moneyed man, the misanthrope,
> The strongest that the earth has known,
> The subtle worker in the atom world,
> None can hold back the Spring.
> It comes by God's appointment, and His covenant
>   stands
> As it has always stood.

W. SCOTT MORTON

(*Thanksgiving and Praise*)

To all of us the gift of Spring means much, but to the Christian heart it means most of all.

> 'Tis the Spring of souls today;
> Christ hath burst His prison,
> And from three days' sleep in death
> As a sun hath risen;
> All the winter of our sins,
> Long and dark, is flying
> From His light, to whom we give
> Laud and praise undying.

Trans. J. M. NEALE

(*Praise*)

When Jesus came to walk the ways of earth, winter lay over Nature—and over the hearts of men.

When He left the earth, it was Springtime, life from apparent death was everywhere—and most of all realized in the hearts of men.

In the place where he was crucified there was a garden.   JOHN 19:41

And every garden since, to faithful hearts, is a reminder of the miracle of the first Easter Day.

MATTHEW 28:1-20

Jesus lives! No longer now can thy terrors, Death, appal us!

I will recall how men and women of the early Church rejoiced in this great certainty.

(ACTS 2:31-2, 4:33, 13:30, 17:31)

From the fact of Christ's Resurrection, we move gladly to belief in our own.

The words of Jesus are: 'Because I live, ye shall live also.'   JOHN 14:19

Paul's words are: 'Never forget "Jesus Christ risen from the dead".'   2 TIMOTHY 2:8 (Moffatt)

(*Praise*)

If Jesus died,
Naught but the winter and the gloom remain.
But Jesus lives!
Then full and fain,
Laugh and sing, ye golden flowers,
Drifting clouds and dancing showers.
Christ is risen! Christ is risen!
God's green spring is true again!

Eternal God, who art the Giver of life, I praise Thee for the wonder of the world made new in the Spring of the year, for every daffodil that bursts its prison house in the mould, for every glint and colour of gold. Year by year Thou dost renew this miracle of life before my eyes. Let me never lose the wonder of it.

Above all, I praise Thee for the Resurrection life of Jesus, made manifest in a garden when faithful hearts came seeking at the dawn of the day.

I praise Thee for Death overcome, for Life made new. Let me live daily in the wonder and power of my Risen Lord, who, conquering Death, lives now for evermore. *Amen.*

MY RESPONSE

'At the Cross-roads of Choice'—*Guidance*

'At the Cross-roads of Choice'— Guidance

> *He will teach us of his ways, and we will walk in his paths.* MICAH 4:2
>
> *(Meditation)*

THE PICTURE

No matter how clever our minds, how wise our hearts, how wide our experience, we come time and again to the cross-roads of choice.

(Silence)

Of old, prophets and psalmists depended on God for guidance.

Saints and scholars of our day do the same.

(Recollection)

Dr J. Scott Lidgett, full of years, called his auto-biography: *My Guided Life.*

(Recollection)

Sir Ernest Baker, sometime Principal of King's College, London, looking back, said: 'My life has been shaped for me by a guidance which came to me from outside. . . . So I must need give thanks. . . .'

(*Recollection*)

The conditions of such guidance are—

> I must utterly trust my Guide.
> I must be travelling His way.
> I must be open to receive guidance.
> I must be ready to follow the guidance given.

(*Meditation*)

I will remember the ways in which God's guidance comes.

> Isaiah, in the vivid way of the prophet, may have over-simplified it when he said: 'Thine ears shall hear a word behind thee, saying, This is the way, walk ye in it.' But some seem to have found it as simple as that. 'I hear His whisper in my heart,' said John Wesley.
>
> Some of us, at times, have missed God's guidance, because we have been waiting for something similarly dramatic. 'God, as I see this matter of guidance,' said Dean Matthews, 'does not put the right ideas into our heads; but if we are in communion with Him, He purifies our minds and motives so that we are able to arrive at the right ideas through the faculties which He has given us.'

(*Recollection*)

God guides me through others who have passed this way—

> When Mildred Cable came to the last oasis before

the Gobi Desert, she hesitated. 'But other people have crossed, and left tracks,' said her camel driver. 'If I lose them, the camels will find them; at night-time there will be stars, and they cannot mis-lead us. Have no fear, rest your heart, lady, there will be a road.'

(*Meditation*)

God guides me in active consultation with friends and associates who love and serve—

(*Meditation*)

God guides me through prayer, as I wait reverently and expectantly, ready for action.

The spirit, if not the expression of the old saint of whom Quiller-Couch has told must be mine: 'I sticks my hands in my pockets, an' waits on the Lord; an' what He tells me to do, I do.'

God guides me through a thoughtful and eager reading of His Word, as I ask—

What can I learn from this? What more of Himself is He showing me? Does this rebuke, or challenge me? Does it call for action, or confession, or re-dedication?

God guides me through an enlightened conscience—

(*Recall instances*)

God guides me in worship through the word of a preacher, or a hymn or prayer—

(Recall instances)

But I don't need guidance on most things. 'Over wide areas of life', as Dr Sangster reminds us, 'God has made His will already clear. There are the Ten Commandments. There are our Lord's laws of Love. The ethical standards of the New Testament are plain to anyone who will read the Book. . . . God won't set the Commandments aside to answer a bit of special pleading.'

(Meditation)

MY RESPONSE

'Life's Precious Gift'—A Little Child

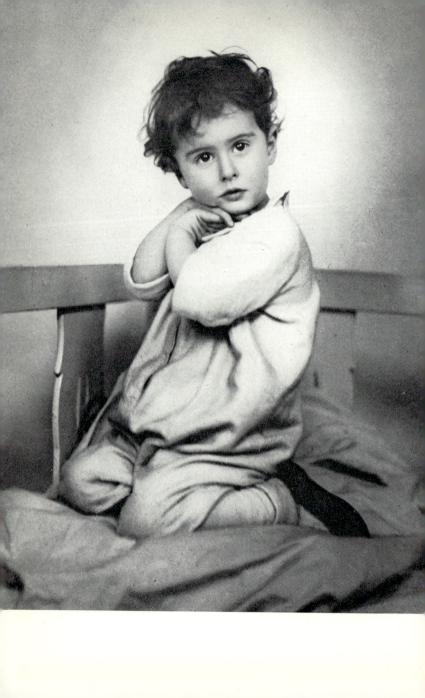

'Life's Precious Gift'—A Little Child

A little child is infinitely precious.

JOHN HALDANE

Of all created things the loveliest
And most divine are children. Nothing here
Can be more *precious* or more dear.

WM. CANTON

(*Silence*)

Once, people saw the value of children much less clearly, because they knew much less about God.

Abraham, a good father, felt God wanted him to kill his son, and lay him on an altar.

GENESIS 22:1-19

Over and over again parents were puzzled—thinking of God only in tribal or national events—outside the daily values of human life.

(*Meditation*)

Then a little child was born in Bethlehem—and what a difference He made!

So little He was, that His mother wrapped Him in

swaddling clothes; so human, that she laid Him in a manger; so divine, that the angels sang over Him!

LUKE 2:1-52

At the time, the three great peoples were the Romans, the Greeks, the Jews.

Roman law required a father to bring up all his sons and his first daughter; beyond that, exposure and infanticide were permissible, and in the case of the puny or mis-shapen, were a duty.

Among the Greeks, small families were favoured, and the abandoning of infants was a commonplace. Aristotle, for all his lofty thought, recommended abortion and exposure.

Jewish parents acknowledged themselves answerable to God for family-life; and though they treated their children with strictness, it was tempered with affection. 'From their swaddling clothes they were trained to recognize God as Father, and Creator of the world.'

(*Meditation*)

Against this background, it is a joy to remember the attitude of Jesus to little children.

In setting values for the disciples. MARK 9:33-7

What did He mean—in modern terms?

In receiving the mothers of Salem. MARK 10:13-16

The simple happenings of that crowded day will never be forgotten to the end of Time.

And on other occasions. MATTHEW 18:3-4, 10

The warning He issued was not only against hurting a child, but against thinking lightly of it.

MATTHEW 11:16-17

(Meditation)

'Almost all the higher religions', Dr Sangster reminds us, 'teach the value of human personality, but Christianity teaches it most clearly of all.'

So I will give thanks for little children.

(Naming those specially dear to me.)

I will give thanks for good parents, and all who aid them—teachers, relations, neighbours, play-mates.

(Naming some, out of special gratitude.)

I will pray for all children handicapped—by hard circumstances, ill-health, lack of understanding, divided homes. *(Naming them as I have knowledge of them.)*

I will pray for children of other lands—with all their differences, as precious as those known to me. (My missionary reading and giving will quicken this petition into life.)

(Silence)

I will pray for good judgement, for wisdom and unselfishness, in dealing with children.—Especially will I pray for love—and joy.

(Silence)

'I believe Jesus is saying (to borrow Dr Donald Soper's words): "Make a world fit for little children to live in

25

—little children of every colour and continent—and then you will have a world fit for everybody else to live in. . . ."

'When every little child has enough to eat, time to say prayers, and nothing much to be afraid of if it hears a bang in the darkness of the night, then will be fulfilled the words of the age-old song: "Peace on earth and good-will among men." '

MY RESPONSE

'The Straight Furrow'—Dedication

'The Straight Furrow'—
Dedication

No man [said Jesus], having put his hand to the plough and looking back, is fit for the Kingdom of God.

LUKE 9:62

(Meditation)

God is saying something to me—

—through this purposeful picture . . .
—through every ploughman who sets hands to the plough and feet in the furrow.

(Recollection)

The simple epitaph of a farm labourer in Ganton reads: 'He ploughed *a straight furrow.*' The words seem to carry a New Testament sense of purposefulness and dedication.

(Meditation)

I will give thanks—

> For the first man to climb the hill
> And seek a prospect wider still;
> For the first man to brave the sea
> Unscared by its immensity;

For he, who, conquering craven fear,
First found in fire a friend to cheer;
Wrought tool and weapon of his own;
For those, the first with patient toil
To break the clod and till the soil;
For all such men, since men began,
I thank the God who made the man.

LILIAN COX

(Thanksgiving)

'The sight of the ploughman at work, the brown field, the gulls circling round the plough, the stillness of the countryside, with this one little human being working in it, the general atmosphere of slowness, patience, breadth and peace—all this uplifts and steadies the mind of the watcher in a wonderful way. The ploughman is not just a man doing a job for himself, or his master, but is part of the great, universal, changeless order of nature, earth, sky, wind and rain, and the never-failing turn of the seasons. . . . He is a man concentrating on the task in hand, but relying on certain changeless realities.

'And that is the Christian life.'

J. NEVILLE WARD

(Meditation)

In the day of Jesus, the ploughman had no polished plough-share, leaving the deep, clean furrow in its wake; his plough was scarcely more than a stout two-pronged pointed stick. But the absurdity of ploughing a straight furrow while looking back remains.

Richard Hengist Horne understands Christ's words —and the challenge of them—when he says: 'Plough deep and straight with all your powers.'

John Oxenham understands them when he says—

> Who answers Christ's insistent call
> Must give himself, his life, his all,
> Without one backward look.
> Who sets his hand upon the plough,
> And glances back with anxious brow,
> His calling hath mistook.
> Christ claims him wholly for His own;
> He must be Christ's, and Christ's alone.

(*Meditation*)

The ploughman is seldom a man of words; he depends on actions for his witness. In the final summing-up, a Christian must do the same.

'How few spoken prayers', says R. Ellis Roberts, 'are as fine as the direct beauty of a straight furrow.'

(*Silence*)

MY PRAYER

Gracious Lord and Master, who hast called me into discipleship, grant me power to plough a straight furrow.

Forgive me that ever the purposefulness of my life has lacked joy; forgive me that others have not always seen in me the stripped beauty of dedication.

In Thy power uphold all who falter; all who, having set their hands to the plough, look back; all who fall to the attraction of an easier way; all who are clever and popular, and to whom most things come easy.

Give strength to those who, continuing in the way, have lost some of the glad purposefulness with which they set out.

Bless those who must move among strangers; grant Thy special blessing to all who are young and inexperienced in discipleship.

And keep us, young and old alike, responsive to Thy glorious call, and faithful till our life here is done.

Amen.

(*Silence*)

MY RESPONSE

He that ploweth should plow in hope.

I CORINTHIANS 9:10

'The Many-splendoured Thing'—Vision

'The Many-splendoured Thing'
—Vision

> 'Tis ye, 'tis your estrangèd faces,
> That miss the *many-splendoured thing*.

(Meditation)

THE PICTURE

I will wait for what God has to say to me through this striking picture.

The man—eyes at a low level—misses the surprising beauty of the spire of St Martin-in-the-Fields mirrored in the shower-drenched street.

(Silence)

What 'many-splendoured thing' am I missing at this moment?

Some God-given gift near at hand? Some glimpse of Nature—of craftsmanship—of human courage —self-giving—generosity?

(Silence)

To seek out such riches, and to make response, is one of the things which puts me above the beasts of the field.

In this silence, I will remember that

> —Moses found the burning-bush in the familiar place of his work   EXODUS 3:1-22

> —Jacob saw the ladder ascending to heaven from where he laid down his head to rest
>   GENESIS 28:10-22

> —The young man discovered the very mountain he thought he knew well to be full of horses and chariots of the Lord   2 KINGS 6:15-17

> —The shepherds in the fields, as on a hundred other nights, saw a sight never before granted to men   LUKE 2:8-16

In this silence, I will recollect that—to each of these, 'the many-splendoured thing' was a new revelation of God.

(Meditation)

Said the Proverb-maker: 'The eyes of a fool are in the ends of the earth'   PROVERBS 17:24

(Meditation)

Is it foolishness of this kind that Henry Ward Beecher has to confess?—'Eyes I had, but I did not see; now I see marvellous things. Ears I had, but I did not hear. Now I hear things that are wonderful beyond all description.'

(Meditation)

How could men and women walk and talk with Jesus day after day, and not see in Him the supreme revelation of God?

32

> With eyes at earth-level, they said: 'Is not this the
> carpenter's son? is not his mother called Mary?
> and his brethren, James, and Joses, and Simon,
> and Judas? And his sisters, are they not all with
> us?'   MATTHEW 13:55-6, LUKE 3:23, 4:22

I will ponder what God is saying to me, through a
    poet of today—

Joses, the brother of Jesus, was only a worker in wood,
And he never could see the glory that Jesus, his brother,
    could.
'Why stays he not in the workshop?' he often used to
    complain,
'Sawing the Lebanon cedar, imparting to woods their
    stain?
Why must he go thus roaming, forsaking my father's
    trade,
While hammers are busily sounding, and there is gain
    to be made?'
Thus ran the mind of Joses, apt with plummet and
    rule,
And deeming whoever surpassed him either a knave
    or a fool—
For he never walked with the prophets of God's great
    garden of bliss.
And of all the mistakes of the ages, the saddest, me-
    thinks, was this—
To have such a brother as Jesus, to speak with Him
    day by day,
And never to catch the vision which glorified His clay.

(Meditation)

I will try to see what hindered the vision—

    Of Joses (MARK 3:21, margin)
    Of Nathanael (JOHN 1:45-51)
    Of the woman at the well (JOHN 4:4-26)
    Of John the Baptist (LUKE 7:19-23)
    Of Thomas (JOHN 20:24-31)

                (*Meditation*)

MY PRAYER

    O Lord, that I might receive my sight,
    And nevermore be blind
    To the sheen upon the wild-bird's breast,
    To the glory of gold in the sun-drenched west,
    To the hurt that is hidden in secret deep,
    The holy courage a heart can keep;
    To the wonder of faith, the glory of love,
    And the infinite mercy of God above,
    May I never more be blind!

MY RESPONSE

34

'For the Anxious Heart'—*Trust*

'For the Anxious Heart'—Trust

Behold the birds . . . [said Jesus], they sow not, neither do they reap, nor gather into barns; and your heavenly Father feedeth them. Are not ye of much more value than they?   MATTHEW 6:26 RV

(Silence)

'Why are you anxious? Your heavenly Father knoweth', said He.

(Silence)

Jesus felt at home in a universe where His Father undertook even for sparrows   LUKE 12:6

(Silence)

Anxiety, calculating care, assumes total responsibility for one's needs—and forgets God. The birds fulfil their own nature—and God does His own great part.

(Meditation)

'Jesus meant no encouragement to idleness when He said that God who fed the sparrows and clothed the lilies would feed and clothe us. Sparrows in fact work hard for their food. Yet it is God who feeds them, and when they die it is not without the Father, as Jesus said.

35

Nor was Jesus discouraging reasonable forethought and planning when He told us not to worry about to-morrow. Anxious fears about what we cannot control are not the same as intelligent forethought and co-operative planning for the common good.'

DR HUGH MARTIN

(*Meditation*)

The poet, W. H. Auden, says that this age could well be called 'The Age of Anxiety'.

Does that mean that we have forgotten Christ's words about the Father—and must fall back on aspirins, phenobarbitone, luminal?

A simple poem poses that question—

> Said the Robin to the Sparrow:
>   'I should really like to know
> Why these anxious human beings
>   Rush about and worry so.'

> Said the Sparrow to the Robin:
>   'Friend, I think that it must be
> That they have no heavenly Father
>   Such as cares for you and me.'

(*Silence*)

God is saying something to me through this beautiful picture—

God is saying something to me through the seeing eye of the poet—

It wins my admiration
To view the structure of that little work,
A bird's nest. Mark it well within, without!
No tool had he who wrought, no knife to cut,
No nail to fix, no bodkin to insert,
No glue to join: his little beak was all—
And yet how neatly finished! What nice hand,
With every implement and means of art,
And twenty years' apprenticeship to boot,
Could make me such another?

WILLIAM HURDIS

(Silence)

—Said Warren Seabury, having looked long and often
at the birds, and pondered the words of Jesus—

'I do not know what is before me, but I am building
my nest in the greatness of God.'

(Meditation)

Said Elizabeth Barrett Browning, after much experience of life—

Oh, the little birds sang east, and the little birds sang
west,
And I smiled to think God's greatness flowed around
our incompleteness—
Round our restlessness, His rest.

(Meditation)

Said Alistair McLean, in this Age of Anxiety—

'I lose myself in wonder as I watch the sky. I bow

before the wisdom of Thy law which gives the star its course, and the bird its nest.'

(*Meditation*)

Said Romany, the BBC Nature-man, as he expressed his thanks in prayer—

'O God, our Father . . . Thou dost come to us in a thousand ways. Thou dost speak to some through the loveliness of the world about us—the colour of it, with the budding hedgerows, and the song of birds. . . . We thank Thee for the alphabet of Thy love.'

MY PRAYER

'A Bridge in the Background'—Understanding

'A Bridge in the Background'—Understanding

'No one can say who built the first bridge . . . after a twisted vine, a ready-made bridge consisting of a fallen tree-trunk lying across a stream.

'Those were the very first bridges.'   ARTHUR MEE

(Silence)

Then came simple man-made bridges, and splendid stone bridges built by the Romans; and others followed their lead.

Now it is impossible to conceive of steady progress up through the long years, without a bridge in the background.

(Recollection)

As a general pored over a map, his staff-officer indicated a line of advance by moving his finger quickly across the map. But suddenly the general said: 'Stop! Your finger is not a bridge!'

THE PICTURE

—God is saying something to me through this strong, graceful bridge over the Thames at Clifton Hampden —linking Berkshire with Oxfordshire.

The little fishermen are wholly absorbed—but no one can grow to adulthood without concern for 'a bridge in the background'.

(Meditation)

John Buchan used to say: 'I am a great bridge man'—meaning: I like leaning over a bridge, with a contented mind, while the water glides beneath.'

But there is much more to it.

Bridges are for linking people together—man with man, east with west, the 'haves' with the 'have-nots'.

(Meditation)

An old man, going a lone highway,
Came at the evening, cold and grey,
To a chasm, vast and deep and wide,
Through which was flowing a sullen tide.
The old man crossed in the twilight dim,
The sullen stream had no fears for him;
But he turned when safe on the other side
And built a bridge to span the tide.

'Old man,' said a fellow pilgrim near,
'You are wasting strength with building here;
Your journey will end with the fading day,
You never again may pass this way;
You have crossed the chasm, deep and wide—
Why build you the bridge at eventide?'

The builder lifted his old grey head:
'Good friend, in the path I have come,' he said,

'There followeth after me today
A youth whose feet must pass this way.
He, too, must cross in the twilight dim;
Good friend, I'm building the bridge for him.'

ANON

(Thanksgiving)

When he broadcast his first message as President of the Methodist Church of Great Britain, Dr Leslie Weatherhead said: 'I want in my year of office to be a bridge-builder . . . to bridge the gulf that separates us from those lovable, attractive, often very fine people who are estranged from the churches.

'We need what they can give . . . and they need what we can give them.'

(Meditation)

Dr J. B. Webb, President of the South African Methodist Conference, said lately: 'We believe that our job is to continue with our positive witness, and to build as many "bridges" as we can, in the situation in which we find ourselves.'

(Meditation)

I will recall, in the presence of God, some of the things that separate me from others—

Ignorance
Fear
Pride
Suspicion
Prejudice

And in the larger world—
   Racial superiority
   The caste system
   Illiteracy
   Political propaganda
   National greed

'How badly we need bridges! Bridges mean fellowship . . . it is the lack of fellowship that is spoiling our world.'

(*Meditation*)

The materials for bridge-building are
   Love
   Accurate information
   Friendliness
   Disinterested service
   Generosity

(*Dedication*)

There is a bridge, whereof the span
Is rooted in the heart of man,
And reaches without pile or rod,
   Unto the Great White Throne of God.

GILBERT THOMAS

MY RESPONSE

'Our Daily Bread'—Provision

'Our Daily Bread'—Provision

The promise is: 'Seed-time and harvest shall not cease.'

GENESIS 8:22

(Silence)

'God cares about our humble personal needs. He does not expect us to pretend that we do not.'

DR HUGH MARTIN

THE PICTURE

This simple picture reminds me of the unending goodness of God.

(Recollection)

Richard Jefferies, surveying the corn-fields in early Spring, sees: 'Everywhere larks singing their eager welcome away across the plains to the downs and up on the highest hill. Every crust of English bread', says he, 'has been sung over, at its birth in the green blade, by a lark.'

(Thanksgiving)

'The world has seen the passing of many civilizations; but the harvest, which God ordained before any of them, has outlasted them all.

'The world has seen many wicked men; but the sun and the rain have not ceased to fertilize their fields.

'So the love of God endures through all time and all evil; nothing can stop Him from expressing it.'

JOHN ARNOLD

(Thanksgiving)

And yet millions starve.

No prayer rises from the earth so continuously as the prayer for bread.

'The question of bread for myself is a material question, but the question of bread for my neighbour, for everybody, is a spiritual question.' NICOLAS BERDYAEV

(Meditation)

In this world of seasons, work, sun, showers and ingatherings, there is enough for all—but only as we live under one Father, as one family.

Our economy breaks down at the point where our inward relationship with our Father and our brother breaks down.

Our Lord taught us to pray: '*Our* Father . . . *our* daily bread.'

MATTHEW 6:11

(Meditation)

'There is a healthy materialism about Christianity.'

Our Lord's teaching did not deal with other-worldly sentiments for the well-satisfied; it dealt with bread—and now.

He was tempted by the need of it in the wilderness

MATTHEW 4:1-11

He fed five thousand—as well as talked to them.
MATTHEW 14:15-21

At the Last Supper, He took bread, and brake it,
and shared it. MATTHEW 26:17-30

He joined two as they walked to Emmaus, and
in the act of breaking bread they recognized
Him. LUKE 24:13-31

When He searched for a word that would express
His power to satisfy the whole of life's need,
He said: 'I am the living bread which came
down from heaven: if any man eat of this
bread, he shall live for ever.' JOHN 6:51

'Man does not live by bread alone; but without it he
does not live at all.'

(*Meditation*)

MY PRAYER

I thank Thee, Lord, for strength of arm
To win my bread,
And that, beyond my need is meat
For friend unfed:
I thank Thee, Lord, for bread to live,
I thank Thee more for bread to give.

I will give thanks for—

All who plough and sow—in peasant conditions,
and in the immense spreading fields of mechanized
countries.

For all who reap laboriously under the blistering
sun, or seated upon a machine.

For all who link the prayer of our Lord with the sharing of harvest.

I will give thanks for—

All who mill and market corn, fairly and justly.

For all who make bread—and distribute it.

For all mothers and fathers who toil to earn it.

I will give thanks for—

The surprising ways in which God answers His children's needs.

'I was coming home after a long tramp', said Canon Charles Raven, a while ago, 'and passed a dingy shop. . . . The place was lit with naphtha flares, and misty with the steam of cooking; and the smell of damp humanity and food was heavy in the air.

'And again of a sudden there was the glory—God, fulfilling His eternal task, giving His children their daily bread.'

(*Thanksgiving*)

'Without God, we cannot feed the world; without us, God will not.'

'*Through a Green Glade*'—*Refreshment*

'Through a Green Glade'—Refreshment

God is here! I hear His voice
While thrushes make the woods rejoice!

MADELEINE AARON

(*Silence*)

THE PICTURE

Through this peaceful picture, God is recalling to me times of refreshment—and promising others.

(*Silence*)

'Come unto me', said our Lord, 'and I will refresh you.'   MATTHEW 11:28, Moffatt

His offer still holds . . .

(*Meditation*)

'Come away by yourselves to some lonely spot, and get a little rest.'   MARK 6:31, Moffatt

(*Meditation*)

He did not say 'Go!' He said 'Come!' And still He accompanies those who respond to His call.

(*Meditation*)

Am I too busy to hear Him say that?

(Silence)

A disciple in our own day underlines His secret.

'Remember', says Evelyn Underhill, 'that all life comes to you from God, and is to be used for Him—so live in it all, and get the necessary variety and refreshment, without which religious intensity soon becomes stale and hard.'

I will make confession—

Of those times lately when I have failed to hear His call: 'Come . . . rest!'

I will ask forgiveness—

For an over-crowded diary . . . for feverish activity . . . for self-importance . . . for fussiness.

I will give thanks—

For occasional breathing-spaces amidst life's strenuous tasks . . .

I will recall—

The beauty of Nature . . . grass beneath my feet . . . green wooded places . . . the healing warmth of the sun . . . the sky . . .

I will praise God—

For human fellowship—for all with whom I can be silent—and understood.

(Meditation)

But Nature's green glade can never meet my deepest need. Nature is but the 'garment of God'—not His heart. And only His heart, revealed in the life, death, and rising again of His Son, and today in His living presence, is enough.

To find refreshment that matches my need, I must know deeply

> His forgiveness
> His restoration
> His power
> His peace
> His joy

Dr Faber underlines this secret, so that now I can sing it—

> O wide-embracing, wondrous love,
> We read Thee in the sky above,
> We read Thee in the earth below,
> In seas that swell, and streams that flow.

> We read Thee in the flowers, the trees,
> The freshness of the fragrant breeze,
> The songs of birds upon the wing,
> The joy of summer and of spring.

But—

> We read Thee best in Him who came
> To bear for us the Cross of shame,
> Sent by the Father from on high,
> Our life to live, our death to die.

(Meditation)

Gracious Lord, deliver me from myself. Take my limping will, and quicken it to do Thy bidding; take my wilting thoughts, and refresh them by Thy grace; let Thy peace possess me, and Thy beauty be seen in my bearing, as I go about the common affairs of life.

I would remember before Thee all those who have no green glades to remember, all who struggle on without seeking Thy grace. I would remember before Thee those who do not pray for themselves, all who fill up their lives with feverish comings and goings, all whose conscious moments are centred on material things.

Give Thy strength to those whose days are spent on demanding tasks, dull tasks, dangerous tasks.

Grant Thy full salvation to those who feel the fascination of forbidden things, Thy quiet peace and keeping to those whose nerves are frayed, whose bodies are burdened and weary. In Thy presence, let us each find refreshment. *Amen.*

MY RESPONSE

'Above the Low Levels of Life'—Aspiration

'Above the Low Levels of Life' —Aspiration

The heights of the hills are his also.

PSALM 95:4, Margin

In *Mountain Top*, F. S. Smythe wrote: 'Alone amidst Nature, a man learns to be one with all, and all with One.'

When news of his early death reached his friends in the mountains, they said: 'Smythe was a lover of the rare gifts of God, above the low levels of life.'

(Meditation)

Can I enter into his secret?

It is something more than skis and climbing-kit; it belongs to the spirit.

There is a challenge in Smythe's own words: 'The force that drives man toward the summit of the highest hills is the same force that has raised him above beasts. He is not put into this world merely to exist; he is put here to find happiness, to express and to create.'

(Meditation)

Circumstances have seemingly little to do with it.

Sir John Hunt reminds us, in the finishing words of

his great epic, *The Ascent of Everest:* 'There is no height that the spirit of man, guided by a Higher Spirit, cannot attain.'

(Silence)

Dr Alexander Whyte, the beloved preacher, was born illegitimate. He had everything against him—yet how he climbed! (Recall his life-story by G. F. Barbour.)

Helen Keller had everything against her. A little child blind, deaf, dumb, unhappy, unmanageable—she might have grovelled. She chose instead to climb. And today, her spirit walks free in the ampler spaces, her life and serving clothed with a rare dignity. (*I will re-read her life-story.*)

Gladys Aylward, the little parlour-maid, with the call of China in her heart, had, it must have seemed to those beside her, everything against her—no funds, no training. Yet her life-story is one of the most amazing in our time. (*I will re-read 'The Small Woman' by Alan Burgess.*)

Florence Allshorn, choice soul, founder of St Julian's Community, is another. (*I will re-read her story by J. H. Oldham.*)

Aud there are others—God is continually speaking through them.

(Recollection)

Unto the hills around do I lift up
    My longing eyes;

O whence for me shall my salvation come,
    From whence arise?
From God the Lord doth come my certain aid,
From God the Lord who heaven and earth hath made.

He will not suffer that thy foot be moved;
    Safe shalt thou be:
No careless slumber shall his eyelids close
    Who keepeth thee.
Behold, He sleepeth ne'er,
Who keepeth Israel in His holy care.

Jehovah is Himself thy keeper true,
    Thy changeless shade;
Jehovah thy defence on thy right hand
    Himself hath made.
And thee no sun by day shall ever smite;
No moon shall harm thee in the silent night.

From every evil shall He keep thy soul,
    From every sin;
Jehovah shall preserve thy going out,
    Thy coming in.
Above thee watching, He whom we adore
Shall keep thee henceforth, yea, for evermore.
(Paraphrase by JOHN CAMPBELL, Duke of Argyle,
                        1845-1914)

(*Meditation*)

I will make time for worship—

    since it lifts me above the beasts of the field—
    above the low 'levels of life'.

I will give thanks for home—

> not least for the challenge that each day brings—
> for the need to offer there daily my 'utmost for
> the Highest'.

I will acknowledge my place in the community—

> though it lays burdens upon my shoulders, and
> calls for unselfish living.

(Silence)

> Thou hast sent the trackless winds
>   Loose upon their way;
> Thou hast reared a coloured wall
>   Twixt the night and day;
> But chief of all Thy wondrous works,
>   Supreme of all Thy plan,
> Thou hast put an upward reach
>   In the heart of man.

MY RESPONSE

'Motherhood'—A Wondrous Ministry

'Motherhood'—A Wondrous Ministry

Only love can kindle
Light that never dies,
And for little children
Sets the sparkle in their eyes.

(*Praise*)

THE PICTURE

As I look at this picture, let me give thanks that it is so near to the heart of things.

(*Thanksgiving*)

Jesus took a little child, and set it in the midst. 'And putting His arms round it said to them, "Whoever receives one of these little ones in my name, receives me, and whoever receives me, receives not me but him who sent me".'   MARK 9:36-7, Moffatt

(*Meditation*)

Can it be that the test of our adult society is in what it does to little children?

(MATTHEW 18:1-6, LUKE 17:2)

From the days of child chimney-sweeps, mine and factory workers, till this hour?

55

Can it be that the test of our home-life is in what it does to little children? PSALM 127:3

What of the number of broken homes, and bewildered little ones?

And must our religion be subjected to the same test? MARK 10:13-16

'Of such is the Kingdom of Heaven', said Jesus. And again: 'Except ye be converted, and become as little children, ye shall not enter into the kingdom of heaven.' MATTHEW 18:3

Childlikeness is not *childishness*. Simplicity, wholeheartedness, trust, joy, eagerness, are marks of childhood.

(*Meditation*)

'On the laugh of a child', says George Russell, 'I am borne to the joy of the King.'

(*Thanksgiving*)

'Do not be afraid of being too happy, or think that you honour God by wearing a sour face', says Kingsley.

(*Thanksgiving*)

Tributes are not lacking—

'To that girl-mother', says Ernest Rhys, joint-editor of the famous Everyman Library, 'I owe my keenest early sensations. Her face was so full of light, set off by her black hair that fell to her feet when uncoiled, the smiling full-lipped mouth, the hazel eyes. . . . And her voice, a light treble, had a girlish ring, and she could sing a cradle song or a London ditty, or an old hymn clear as a silver spoon.'

(*Thanksgiving*)

Professor George Trevelyan, in his foreword to Eleanor Acland's *Goodbye for the Present*, says: 'The story of Ellen told here by her mother is a thing of unsullied beauty, like a meadow at dawn. To try to define its qualities would be a profanation. Let the reader find them for himself.'

(*Thanksgiving*)

'My mother was to me', says the great modern preacher of Riverside Church, Dr Harry Fosdick, 'what no one could have expected or required. I can without irreverence, paraphrase Paul's words: "What the law could not do, God, sending my mother, did for me." '

(*Thanksgiving*)

Once it used to be said: 'Children are a kind of discipline of humanity.' With rare understanding, Nan Fairbrother, a modern mother, elaborates that saying: 'There are so many disciplines in being a parent, besides the obvious ones like getting up in the night, and putting up with the noise in the day. And almost the hardest of all is learning to be a well of affection, and not a fountain; to show them we love them, not when *we* feel like it, but when they do.'

(*Meditation*)

Mother-love is so much more than smother-love.

True love knows nothing of one-way traffic. The child who comes out into life wanting only to be liked by all, without knowing that love comes in response to love, is not well prepared.

MY PRAYER

Lord of Life, there is no good and lovely thing but comes from Thee. I bless Thee for the sacred ties of life which bind heart to heart. I bless Thee for all happy mothers—for their love, and their wisdom not learned in the schools, for the light in their eyes, and the laughter on their lips. I bless Thee for mothers' dependability when ways are strange, for their fellowship when Life poses its questions.

With grateful heart, I remember my own mother.

Bless, I beseech Thee, all young mothers with their children about them. Keep them responsive to the highest, and give them in the daily comings and goings of life, Thine own secret beauty. *Amen.*

(Silence)

What can a mother give her children
　　Greater today than this one great thing,
Faith in an old, sweet, beautiful story,
　　A star, a stable, a newborn King?

'The Hours against the Centuries'—Perspective

'The Hours against the Centuries'—Perspective

'The secret of life is to set the hours against the centuries.'

EMERSON

(Silence)

THE PICTURE

God is saying something through this striking figure of Queen Boadicea of the first century—against the passing hours of Big Ben.

(Meditation)

'The clock indicates the moment—but what does eternity indicate?' asks Walt Whitman.

'When we set the ages over against the hours', says Carroll Simcox, 'and the experience of the race as a whole—past and present—over against our little pocket of creature-comfort, we see the real truth of the matter.'

Perspective is not easily gained.

I will confess—

My self-importance
My endless haste

My love of things material
My short-sighted judgements

(*Silence*)

'Only a generation which has been educated through religion', says Karl Mannheim, the sociologist, 'or, at least on the religious level, to discriminate between immediate advantages and the lasting issues of life, will be capable of accepting the sacrifices which a properly planned democratic order must continually demand.'

(*Meditation*)

PRAYER

O Lord God of time and eternity,
   Who makest us creatures of time,
that when time is over
   we may attain Thy blessed eternity;
With time, Thy gift,
   give us also wisdom to redeem the time,
lest any day of grace be lost;
   For our Lord Jesu's sake. Amen.

CHRISTINA ROSSETTI

(*Meditation*)

'Life in Time remains without meaning', says our modern scholar, Berdyaev, 'if it does not receive its meaning from Eternity.'

What does he mean—in terms of my everyday life?

What things tempt me—in terms of immediate gain?

Let me consider anew the temptations of Jesus.

LUKE 4:1-13

> Bread hard to find.
> Justice hard to come by.
> God hard to know.

PRAYER

> God harden me against myself,
> This coward with pathetic voice
> Who craves for ease and rest and joys.

CHRISTINA ROSSETTI

Jesus went into the wilderness that He might get His life and ministry into perspective. MATTHEW 4:1-11

On occasion, He called His disciples apart from the busy pattern of life, that they might see it in perspective. MARK 6:31

Paul sought the sense of perspective he needed in withdrawal from crowded places and events that pressed heavily. GALATIANS 1:11-17

(*Meditation*)

Some, today, find perspective through experiences of suffering—through sorrow.

'I must pass through the darkness of Good Friday, if He asks it of me, if I would at length reach Easter dawn and live.' LEN HORWOOD

In *The Last Enemy*, Richard Hilary's sensitive story of a young airman, about to die, he shows him being visited by Denise the widow of his friend Peter, who has been killed. 'For a moment', she says, out of strong Christian faith, 'the darkness outside becomes brightness. We have a glimpse of what lies beyond this life. I believe not only in life after death, but in life before death . . . in a state not of being, but of becoming.'

(*Meditation*)

The seen is transient, the unseen eternal.

2 CORINTHIANS 4:18, Moffatt

MY PRAYER

Eternal One, who art from everlasting to everlasting, grant that I may live in Time as in Eternity.

Help me to distinguish between the things which matter and the things which do not matter.

Grant me clear vision that I may never confuse prejudice with principle.

And when at last I lay down this transient life, grant me peace and joy. *Amen.*

'*Beauty in an Unexpected Place*'—*Transformation*

'Beauty in an Unexpected Place'
—Transformation

God's ageless promise is: 'The desert shall rejoice and blossom.'   ISAIAH 35:1

(Meditation)

THE PICTURE

I will look long at this simple picture—and see God's promise come to pass.

(Silence)

In Nevada is the great Boulder Dam—begun in 1931, and finished five years later. Its construction cost millions of tons of material—and eighty-nine lives. Today, bearing their names, a tablet carries the inscription: 'These Died That The Desert Might Bloom.'

(Remembrance)

A desert is usually an endless waste of sand—arid, worthless, full of monotony.

But—

    A desert does not have to be
      A sandy waste where springs are dry;
    A life can shrink to barrenness
      If love goes by.

A desert does not have to be
  A place where buzzards wheel at dawn;
A heart can hold as dreadful things
  When faith is gone.

(*Meditation*)

Mildred Cable traversed the desert—up into the great Gobi, carrying the message of the Eternal, who transforms barrenness into beauty. In *Ambassadors For Christ*, *Something Happened*, and *The Gobi Desert*, it is plain that transformation may not happen easily, or at once; but it is God's doing.

Once Mildred Cable retraced her tracks, and found a simple desert dweller, to whom she had given the message, completely changed. She had given up opium. 'She held herself differently,' said the traveller. 'She led us into a room, and on the wall was a picture which we had formerly given her . . . a flower opening its pure petals toward heaven, though its roots were buried deep. . . . "It is two years since you were here before," said the woman. "I have never smoked opium since then. I could not go on displeasing God!" ' So the desert had begun to blossom.

(*Meditation*)

For every remembrance of such service, for every transformation God effects in unlikely places, I will give thanks.

(*Thanksgiving*)

Dr John Flynn traversed the desert—up into the great

Inland of Australia, ministering to lonely families and cattle-men, in the name of Him who transforms barrenness into beauty. He came too often to hastily-covered graves, post-and-rail memorials, nameless headstones, new graves of mothers who had died in child-birth. So the Flying Doctor Service was begun—and at sacrifice, the desert transformed.

Through reading *Flynn of the Inland*, by Ian Idris, and *Flying Doctor Calling*, by Ernestine Hill, many may now enter into that transformation—*and thank God at every remembrance of it.*

(*Thanksgiving*)

Dr Hastings reminds us: 'There is always something alluring about the transformation of the desert. . . . As in the realm of Nature, so in the sphere of human nature. Our Lord will transform the desert soul, and make it blossom.'

MY PRAYER

Gracious and ever-living God, hear my prayer for all whose lives hold unloveliness, whose springs of mercy are dried up. Draw near them with Thy refreshing power, that love and beauty and service may blossom. (*In my heart I name some of them before Thee.*)

Bless especially with Thy grace all whose days are dull, whose hopes are withered. (*In my heart I name some of them before Thee.*)

Bless all who look expectantly to Thee for what they cannot do for themselves. (*In my heart I name some of them before Thee.*)

Accept, for Thy mercy's sake, the offering of my own heart, the service of my own hands, that I may be a sharer in the transformation of deserts. In the name of Him who transforms all life, hear my prayer. *Amen.*

MY RESPONSE

'Unto Thee, O Lord, do I lift up my soul!'

'Great are the Things of Every Day'—Work

'Great are the Things of Every Day'—Work

Now is the holy not afar
  In temples lighted by a star,
Now that the King has gone this way,
  Great are the things of every day.

(*Thanksgiving*)

THE PICTURE

Here is a man jogging along at his daily work. Jesus also grew up in a working-man's home—

LUKE 2:39-52

He became widely known for his daily work—

MATTHEW 13:53-8

He spoke of yokes— MATTHEW 11:29-30

He spoke of barns— LUKE 12:18

When He laid aside the chisel and the adze and stepped down to the river to be baptized, God spake, saying: 'Thou art my beloved Son; in thee I am well pleased.'

LUKE 3:23

What had He done to please God?

He had not preached a single sermon; He had not told beyond His home circle one of His matchless stories; He had not reached His hand out in healing.

But He had done much; He had been an honest carpenter—made yokes that fitted, tables that stood well, plough-beams that did the work for which they were intended.

(Silence)

Someone has said—

> If Jesus built a ship
> She would travel trim;
> If Jesus roofed a barn
> No leaks would be left by Him.
> If Jesus planted a garden
> He would make it like Paradise:
> If Jesus did my day's work,
> It would delight His Father's eyes.

(Meditation)

What did He mean when He said: 'My father worketh hitherto, and I work'?   JOHN 5:17

(Meditation)

Said an old English character, 'This is my way o' looking at it: there's the sperrit o' God in all things and all times—week-day as well as Sunday—and i' the great works and inventions, and i' the figuring and the mechanics. And God helps us with our head-pieces and our hands as well as with our souls.'

(Meditation)

A man I know has made an altar
Of his factory bench,
And one has turned the counter of his store
Into a place of sacrifice and holy ministry.
A Martha in our midst has made
Her kitchen table a Communion table;
A postman makes his daily round
A walk in the temple of God:
To all these each daily happening
Has come to be a whisper from the lips of God,
And every common circumstance
A wayside shrine.

MY PRAYER

Eternal God, Thou hast fashioned my heart to seek
Thee, and my hands to serve Thee. I bless Thee for
work—once life's penance, now its rich reward.

With each new day I bring Thee my praise. I lie
down to rest with weariness, and with fresh vigour
arise. For the gift of sleep, I bless Thee.

I bless Thee for home, and fire, and food; for friendship, and fun. I bless Thee for the skills that reside in
my hands; for the purposes that employ my mind.

I pray for all who are without work, all who are
discouraged in the work they do, all who are defeated
in themselves—slaves to habits. I pray for all who know
strong temptation: grant them strength to resist; give
them friends to support and to encourage.

Bless all whose energies are set on good under-
takings, all workers in the fields; all apprentices, all
workers in great cities. Bless especially all whose work

is exacting, all whose work is far from home, all whose work is dangerous.

And may the spirit of Him who served Thee so well in humble Nazareth abide with me:

> So shall no part of day or night
> From sacredness be free;
> But all my life, in every step
> Be fellowship with Thee. *Amen*.

RE-DEDICATION

'A Song in Our Hearts'—Joy

'A Song in Our Hearts'—Joy

'When you watch religion at work, you find a morality; when you converse with religion in its thoughtful moods, you find a theology; but when you get to the heart of religion you find a song.'

PERCY AINSWORTH

(*Thanksgiving*)

From early times, men and women, in their search for God and in their discovery of Him, expressed that experience in song.

The song of Moses—

DEUTERONOMY 31:30, 32:1-52

The song of Deborah and Barak—

JUDGES 5:1-12

The song of David— 2 SAMUEL 22:1-51

But the heart of religion is not in the Old Testament—for all the song there—it is in the New.

But it has become impossible to sing the Old Testament songs and psalms as originally sung; always now they are shot through with new meaning. (Psalm 23, for instance.)

(*Recollection*)

The New Testament revelation of God, through Jesus, His Son, begins with song—

> The song of Mary (LUKE 1:46-55)—
>   the *Magnificat*
> The song of Zacharias (LUKE 1:68-79)—
>   the *Benedictus*
> The song of Simeon (LUKE 2:29-32)—
>   the *Nunc Dimittis*

Then, above all earthly song, came the song of the angels, as the shepherds watched their flocks by night.
LUKE 2:8-14

Every Christmas hears the echo of that song—read in the Scriptures, and sung in church, hospital and home.

The best-known, best-loved songs in the world are those of the coming of Christ.

> 'Hark! the herald-angels sing'
> 'O come, all ye faithful'
> 'Angels from the realms of glory'
> 'Christians, awake'
> 'Still the night, holy the night'
> 'Brightest and best'
> 'O little town of Bethlehem'
> 'Cradled in a manger, meanly'
> 'While shepherds watched'

The first Christmas, God chose for the telling of His greatest news, not a sermon, but a song.

(*Thanksgiving and Praise*)

72

'All realities sing', says Coventry Patmore, 'and nothing else will.'

There is enough tragedy in the New Testament to make it the saddest record of all time; yet it is the most joyful.

In parting—(JOHN 15:11)
In loss—(ACTS 2:46-7)
In suffering—(ACTS 5:41)
In prison—(ACTS 16:25)

(*Thanksgiving and Praise*)

And never once through all the years has that note been missing.

'Hymns', says Dr Erik Routley, 'are the folk-song of the Church militant.'

Charles Wesley has enriched the world for us with thousands of hymns. He wrote one twenty-four hours after his conversion, and dictated one on his death-bed.

Year by year, young voices and old join in his advent hymn of joy:

Hark! the herald-angels sing
Glory to the new-born King.

(*Praise*)

Part of a rich heritage, Isaac Watts left us a Christmas favourite:

Joy to the world, the Lord is come:
Let earth receive her King;
Let every heart prepare Him room,
And heaven and nature sing.

73

Joy to the world, the Saviour reigns;
  Let men their songs employ;
While fields and floods, rocks, hills and plains,
  Repeat the sounding joy.

No more let sins and sorrows grow,
  Nor thorns infest the ground;
He comes to make His blessings flow
  Far as the curse is found.

He rules the world with truth and grace,
  And makes the nations prove
The glories of His righteousness,
  And wonders of His love.'

MY RESPONSE

74

'Of His Very Nature'—Compassion

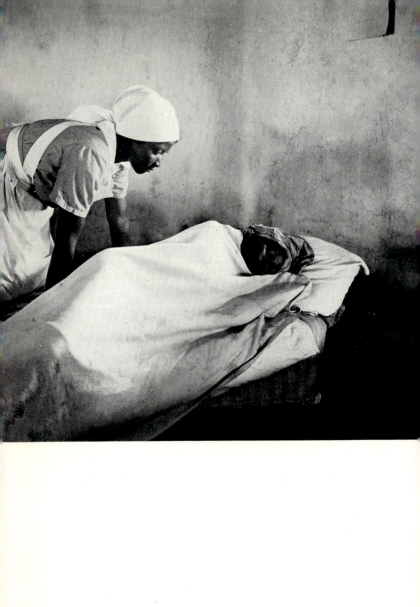

'Of His Very Nature'— Compassion

Thou, O Lord, art a God, full of compassion.

PSALM 86:15

(Silence)

THE PICTURE
God is saying something to me through this quiet, simple picture.

(Silence)

Compassion recognizes no colour-bar.
Compassion recognizes no social status.
Compassion recognizes nothing but need.

(Meditation)

There is comfort in the strength of Love,
It makes a thing endurable which else
Would overset the brain and break the heart!

(Recollection)

'Compassion' is a favourite New Testament word—

Jesus, moved with compassion, put forth his hand.

MARK 1:41

When the Lord saw her, he had compassion on her.

LUKE 7:13

And Jesus had compassion on them, and touched their eyes (MATTHEW 20:34).

And two of His greatest stories centred on compassion:

The story of the Prodigal—
His father had compassion and ran and fell on his neck (LUKE 15:20).

The story of the Good Samaritan—
When he saw him, he had compassion on him, and went to him (LUKE 10:33).

(*Meditation*)

This gracious ministry can never die—

In 1 Peter 3:8, is the word: 'Finally, be ye of one mind, having compassion one of another.'

What does this mean in terms of my everyday life? The dictionary defines 'compassion' as 'Pity, inclining one to spare, or help'. Is that enough?

William Blake asks—

Can I see another's woe,
And not be in sorrow too?
Can I see another's grief,
And not seek for kind relief?

The simple words of another poet are as searching—

Who is so low that I am not his brother?
Who is so high that I've no path to him?
Who is so poor I may not feel his hunger?
Who is so rich I may not pity him?

Who is so hurt I may not know his heartache?
  Who sings for joy my heart may never share?
Who in God's heaven has passed beyond my vision?
  Who in hell's depths where I may never fare?

(Silence)

When a new wing was opened at a Mission Hospital, and dedicated to the gracious memory of a medical man who had given his life in that place, one of the speakers said, as the plaque was unveiled: 'We loved the doctor because he took our hurt into his own heart.'

MY PRAYER

Almighty God, forgive me that I have ever received great benefits from Thy hands with little thanks, and taken for granted Thy rich gifts. I bless Thee for Thy heart revealed in Jesus Christ my Lord—for His holy Love, His strength, His joy, His compassion.

May His Spirit so dwell within me, that my natural understanding and sympathy may be quickened.

Hear me especially for those who make claims upon me—the orphaned and the homeless, the bewildered and the lonely among Thy children. Hear me for all who know the sudden shock of accident, all who suffer disease, or bodily defect.

Grant Thy special grace to those who minister Thy compassion where there is cruelty and greed, where the footprints of fear are in the earth. Bless all who minister to refugees, all who tend lepers in their sore need, all who minister to the sick in mind. Through the long hours when the noises of the day are hushed, be with those on night-duty.

Grant to doctors and nurses, to surgeons and scientists, to laboratory-workers and orderlies a clear sense of responsibility in the discharge of their compassionate ministry. And grant Thy grace of encouragement to men and women everywhere matched against poverty, disease, superstition, and all that hinders a full, glad life; for the sake of our Lord who came to bring Life.

Amen.

MY RESPONSE

Books by Rita F. Snowden

★

LONDON : THE EPWORTH PRESS